NATIONAL GEOGRAPHIC
KIDS™

Just Joking 3

300

hilarious jokes
about everything,
including
tongue twisters,
riddles,
and more!

by Ruth A. Musgrave

NATIONAL
GEOGRAPHIC
WASHINGTON, D.C.

HA! HA! HA! HA! HA! HA! HA! HA! HA! HA! HA! HA! HA! HA! HA! HA! HA!

KNOCK, KNOCK.

Who's there?
Alike.
Alike who?
Alike you,
you're funny!

Dogs' nose-
prints are
as unique
as human
fingerprints.

4

HA!HA!HA!HA!HA!HA!HA!HA!HA!HA!HA!HA!HA!

KNOCK, KNOCK.

Who's there?
Annie Mae.
Annie Mae who?
Annie Mae I have
a cookie?

6

TONGUE TWISTER!

Say this fast three times:

Chet cheated at checkers.

A black-tailed prairie dog greets other prairie dogs by clicking its front teeth together.

Q Why did the submarine captain quit his job?

A Too many ups and downs.

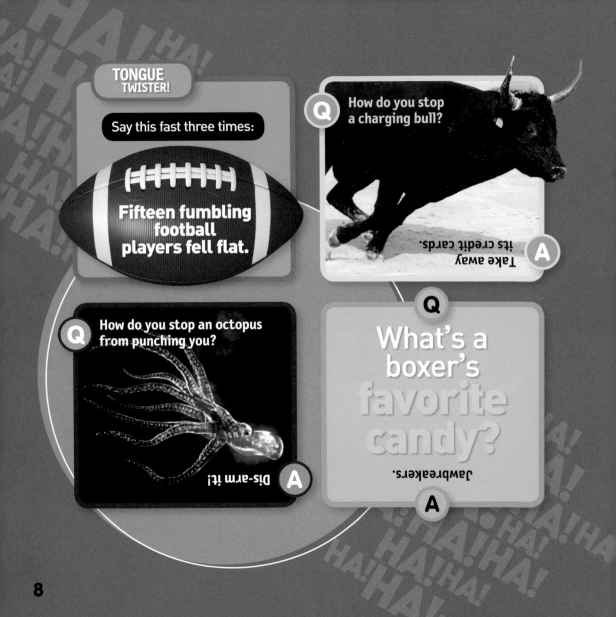

Say this fast three times:

Fifteen fumbling football players fell flat.

Q How do you stop a charging bull?

A Take away its credit cards.

Q How do you stop an octopus from punching you?

A Dis-arm it!

Q

What's a boxer's **favorite candy?**

A Jawbreakers.

8

A harp seal pup grows a layer of blubber by nursing on its mother's high-fat milk.

KNOCK, KNOCK.

Who's there?
Detest.
Detest who?
Detest was so long I almost fell asleep.

10

Live lobsters can be yellow, orange, brown, and even blue.

Q What did the TV say when its remote broke?

A "Help, I'm out of control!"

Q What do you get when you cross a charging rhino?

A Run over!

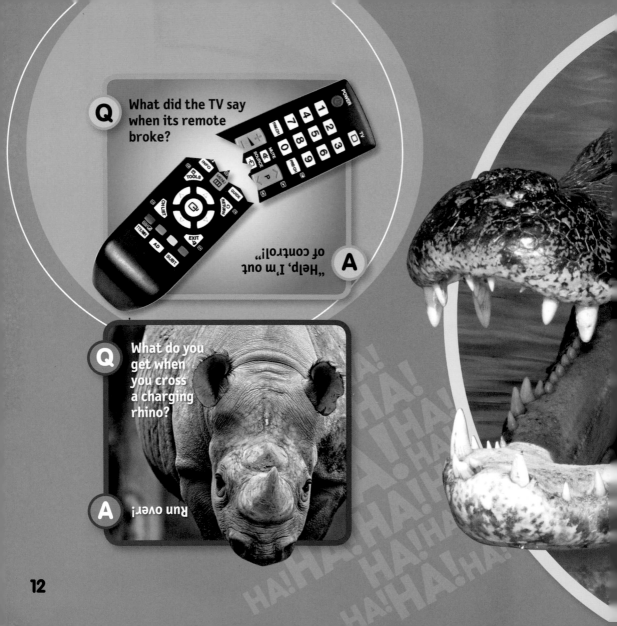

12

The spectacled caiman is named for the ridge that connects its eyes like a pair of spectacles, or glasses.

KNOCK,

KNOCK.

Who's there?
Addle.
Addle who?
Addle be the last time
I knock on your door.

13

Where do **aliens** stay in touch with their friends?

On Spacebook.

Q

Why didn't the **baseball player** score any points?

He kept running home.

A

Q What does the Easter Bunny grow in his garden?

A Eggplants.

Q What's the Tower of Pisa's first name?

A Eileen.

Top chopstick shops stock top chopsticks.

KNOCK, KNOCK.

Who's there?
Ocelot.
Ocelot who?
Ocelot of pizza.
May I have a slice?

This African pit viper's color attracts prey— nectar-loving birds that think it's a flower.

Q What do you call a *cranky GPS?*

A A nag-ivator.

TONGUE TWISTER!

Say this fast three times:

Norse myths.

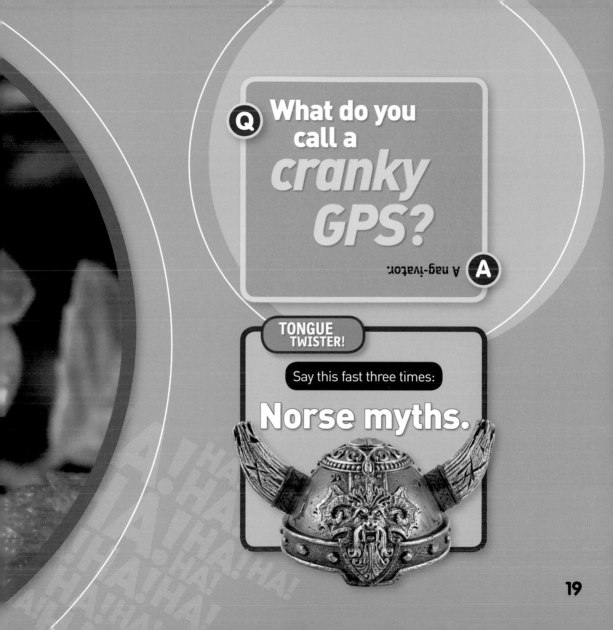

19

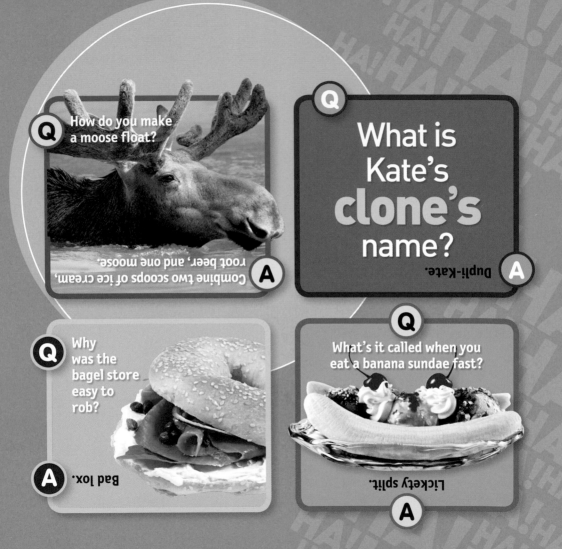

Q How do you make a moose float?

A Combine two scoops of ice cream, root beer, and one moose.

Q What is Kate's **clone's** name?

A Dupli-Kate.

Q Why was the bagel store easy to rob?

A Bad lox.

Q What's it called when you eat a banana sundae fast?

A Lickety split.

21

The American
flamingo has
19 vertebrae in
its neck. Humans
have only 7.

23

Kangaroos can hop up to 25 feet (7.6 m). That's about as far as an Olympic long jumper can leap!

KNOCK, KNOCK.

Who's there?
Selma.
Selma who?
Selma bike, I got a motorcycle!

Q Why did the jellyfish run from every fight?

A It was spineless.

Q Where do **young tigers** swim?

A In the kitty pool.

Q What's it called when a centipede trips?

A Scrambled legs.

Q Why did everyone think the big cat was lazy?

A Because he was always lion around.

Q What do you call the biggest onion ever found?

A A ton-ion.

Q What do you call twin monkeys hanging from a tree limb?

A A swing set.

Q Where do you **watch** people go up and down?

A A stare way.

Q What does a robin open at a picnic?

A A can of worms.

Bonobos sometimes chuckle when tickling each other or playing.

KNOCK, KNOCK.

Who's there?
Aiden.
Aiden who?
Aiden is where a fox lives.

What do you get **when you cross** cocoa **with a** herd of cows?

Chocolate moos.

29

Tokay geckos use sticky hairlike structures on their toes to walk up walls.

KNOCK, KNOCK.

Who's there?
Two-thirds.
Two-thirds who?
Two-thirds, I need a dentist.

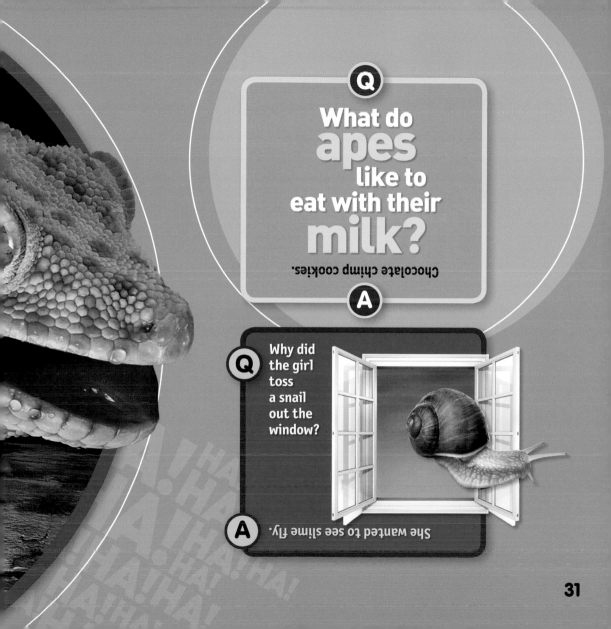

Q

What do apes like to eat with their milk?

A Chocolate chimp cookies.

Q Why did the girl toss a snail out the window?

A She wanted to see slime fly.

31

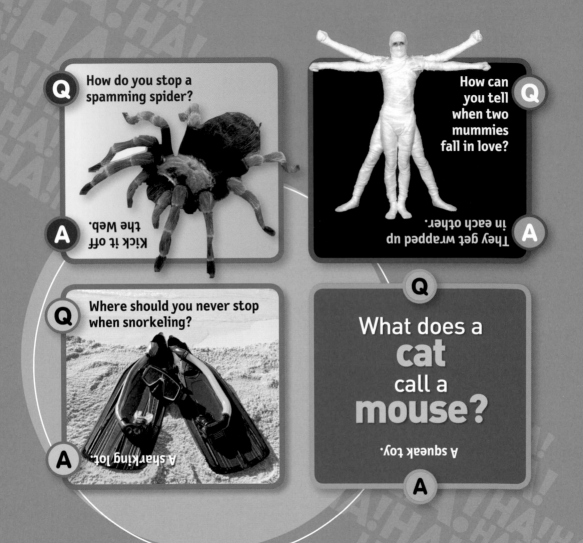

Q How do you stop a spamming spider?

A Kick it off the Web.

Q How can you tell when two mummies fall in love?

A They get wrapped up in each other.

Q Where should you never stop when snorkeling?

A A sharking lot.

Q What does a **cat** call a **mouse?**

A A squeak toy.

KNOCK, KNOCK.

Who's there?
Hammond.
Hammond who?
Hammond eggs.

Badgers use their long claws to carve out burrows and dig for prey.

KNOCK, KNOCK.

Who's there?
Ascot.
Ascot who?
Ascot
to go to the
bathroom.

34

A giraffe's neck is about six feet long. That's as long as some humans are tall.

Where do
pirates
get their morning cup of Joe?

Arrr-bucks.

Q What does an octopus wear when it's cold?

A A coat of arms.

Q Why did the math whiz gain weight?

A Too much pi.

Q What's it called when a **giant** steps on an officer's tent?

A Captain crunch.

TONGUE TWISTER!

Say this fast three times:

Carl quietly quarters cucumbers.

Q What happened to the shark who swallowed a bunch of keys?

A He got lockjaw.

Q What do **Mickey Mouse** and **SpongeBob SquarePants** listen to on the way to work?

A Car tunes.

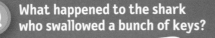

Hippos don't get sunburned because their sweat acts as sunblock.

38

KNOCK,
KNOCK.

Who's there?
Ladybugs.
Ladybugs who?
Ladybugs her husband
to mow the lawn.

39

Ripe white reap ripe white

**wheat reapers
wheat right.**

The regal angelfish has a balloonlike bladder that helps it float.

What is the **best** way to **communicate** with a fish?

Drop it a line.

Q What does a penguin eat for breakfast?

A Ice crispies.

Q What do you do with an old bike?

A Re-cycle it.

Napoleon sent a spy to uncover the enemy's plans. The only place he could hide was in the boot closet. The spy fled before he got any information. When he returned home, Napoleon demanded to know what he had discovered. The spy, refusing to tell a lie, said, "I smelled da-feet!"

French bulldogs originated in England, and later became popular in France.

KNOCK, KNOCK.

Who's there?
Alone.
Alone who?
Alone me a dollar?

44

Q What does it mean if you find a horse shoe?

A Some poor horse is walking around in his socks.

Q

What do you call it when a **cyclops** moves into a **frog's home?**

An eye-pad.

A

T. rex was about as long as a school bus!

47

Q Why did the dolphin quit the deep ocean choir?

A It couldn't reach the low C.

Q Why did the baby bird get into trouble?

Tweet, Tweet,
Tweet, Tweet,
Tweet, Tweet,
Tweet, Tweet,
Tweet, Tweet,
Tweet, Tweet,
Tweet, Tweet.

A It sent too many tweets.

Q Why do **scouts** get stressed when they go **camping?**

A Because their lives are in tents.

Q Where do fish wash?

A In a river basin.

What do you get when you cross a **giraffe** and a **maid?**

Baby giraffes fall five feet to the ground when they are born.

I don't know, but my ceilings have never been so clean.

49

A male donkey is called a jack; a female donkey is called a jenny, or jennet.

KNOCK, KNOCK.

Who's there?
Stopper.
Stopper who?
Stopper, she's running away with your newspaper!

50

Q What do you call a doe caught in a storm?

A A rain deer.

Q What do you call a country where everyone has to drive a red car?

A A red car-nation.

Q What do you take before every meal?

A A seat.

Q What can you **hold** without **ever** touching it?

A A conversation.

51

Great white sharks lose up to 30,000 teeth in a lifetime! New teeth grow to replace them.

What do you get when you cross **a great white shark** with a **computer?**

A mega-bite.

Margays sometimes mimic, or copy, the sounds of their prey.

KNOCK, KNOCK.

Who's there?
Anya.
Anya who?
Anya back is a hairy spider!

Q What does a bee use to cut wood?

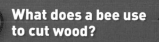

A A buzz saw.

Q

Why did the
dog
cross the road
twice?

He was trying to fetch a boomerang.

A

55

Q What does a surfer get when a big wave hits him in the face?

A Tide-eyed.

Say this fast three times:

Bog dogs blog.

Q Why did the scaredy cat cross the road?

He was a real chicken. **A**

Q Why wasn't the scarecrow ever invited to parties?

A He was a stuffed shirt.

What do you get
when you cross a
magician
and an oak?

Trick or tree.

57

KNOCK, KNOCK.

Who's there?
Mustang.
Mustang who?
Mustang where
that bee
gotcha!

58

If a poodle's coat isn't brushed, it forms ropelike chunks called cords.

The double-crested cormorant grows feather crests above its eyes when it is ready to mate.

KNOCK, KNOCK.

Who's there?
Defense.
Defense who?
Defense is falling over!

60

Frank: One cow, two cows, three cows, four cows...

Hank: What are you doing?
Frank: I'm cownting.

Q

What do you call a **newborn** female plant?

A girl sprout.

A

TONGUE TWISTER!

Say this fast three times:

Dueling dudes duel in the dew.

Q What does a lizard add when it remodels its kitchen?

A Reptiles.

61

Q What happens when you try to **sing** while **eating** a **deli sandwich?**

A You hum a tuna!

TONGUE TWISTER!

Say this fast three times:

Tickle the ticket taker.

Harp seal mothers can identify their pups by smell.

KNOCK, KNOCK.

Who's there?
Eureka.
Eureka who?
Eureka skunk,
take a bath!

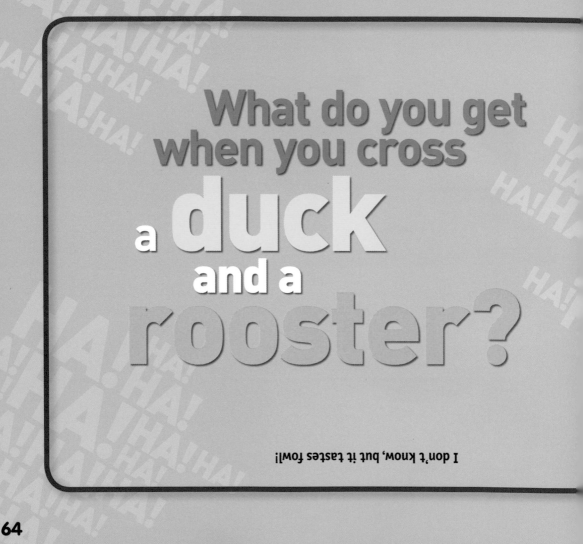

What do you get when you cross a **duck** and a rooster?

I don't know, but it tastes fowl!

A rooster (above) has a rounded beak to grab seeds and insects. A mallard's flat beak (left) filters food from water.

The alpine marmot is considered the largest squirrel species.

KNOCK, KNOCK.

Who's there?
Tennis.
Tennis who?
Tennis a good time to meet.

66

Say this fast
three times:

Shifting shark shadows shocked Sheila.

Q How do you make a clam shut up?

A Take away its shell phone.

67

Q

What did the
tree
wear to the
pool party?

A Swimming trunks.

KATHRYN: You said this cat was good for mice, but he never chases them.

EVA: Well, isn't that good for the mice?

Q How do you know if you've found a prehistoric treasure map?

A T. Rex marks the spot.

Q How do you know when a volcano gets mad?

A It blows its top.

In the wild, chimpanzees like to snack on termites.

Say this fast three times:

Chimp chomps chips.

KNOCK, KNOCK.

Who's there?
Diggity.
Diggity who?
Diggity hole to get to China.

Snow leopards don't roar. They often make a chuff, or puffing sound, when they show aggression.

70

A wolf pack was chowing down on dinner. Suddenly, a pup fell over laughing. His mother looked at the rest of the pack and said, "He must have gotten the funny bone!"

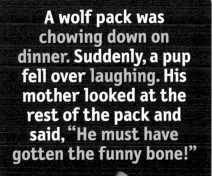

Q How do you know a **zombie** is upset?

A It falls to pieces.

Q Why did the kangaroo mother carry her change in her purse?

A Her pocket was full.

Every tiger's
stripe pattern
is unique.

72

KNOCK, KNOCK.

Who's there?
Satin.
Satin who?
Satin something icky, gotta change my pants.

Q What is Cliff's coatrack called?

A A cliffhanger.

Q What do you call something that smells out of this **world?**

A Heaven scent.

Q What do you name a feline that can't stand up straight?

A Catalina.

What kind of **medicine** does a **vampire** take when he has a **cold?**

Coffin syrup.

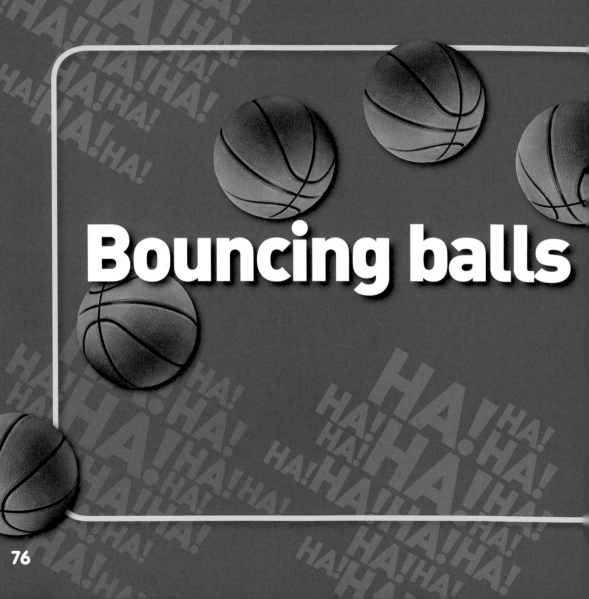

Bouncing balls

bounce off walls.

To keep cool in the desert, fennec foxes radiate body heat from their large ears.

KNOCK, KNOCK.

Who's there?
Ernest.
Ernest who?
Ernest is full of chicks.

78

Q What do you call a parasite that drives a dog crazy?

A A luna-tick.

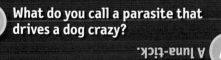

TONGUE TWISTER!

Say this fast three times:

Sally slipped on snail slime.

Q What do you get when you cross a hamster and an automobile?

A A car-pet.

TONGUE TWISTER!

Say this fast three times:

Bamboo baboon.

TONGUE TWISTER!

Say this fast three times:

All aboard, bored boars.

Q What do you call a clumsy letter?

A A bumble B.

A zebra's teeth grow for its entire lifetime. The teeth are worn down by constant chewing and grazing.

KNOCK, KNOCK.

Who's there?
Surpass.
Surpass who?
Surpass the salt, please.

An elephant's trunk contains about 100,000 different muscles.

83

Swans' feathers trap body heat to keep them warm in cold climates.

KNOCK, KNOCK.

Who's there?
Statue.
Statue who?
Statue at the door?

84

Q What's it called when a **mermaid** has to clean her room?

A A sea chore.

Q What do you call a superhero who hates wrinkled clothes?

A Iron man.

Q What does an astronaut use to serve dinner?

A A satellite dish.

Q How did the rabbit win the wrestling match?

A It used a hare pin.

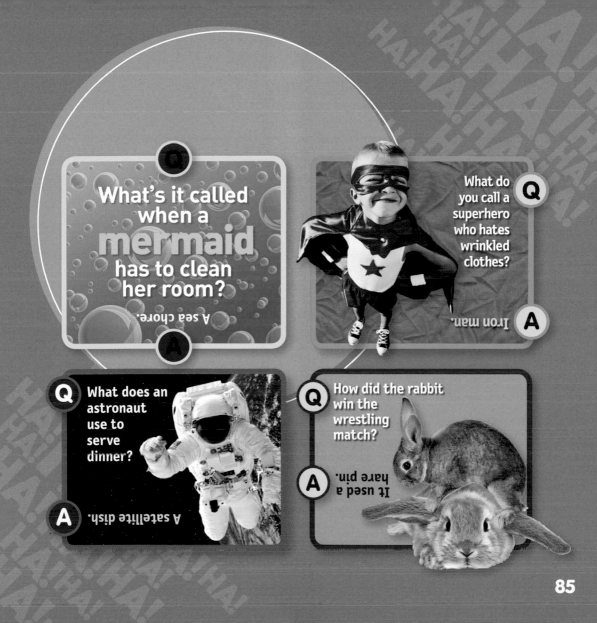

85

Q What's it called when a jouster gets knocked off his horse?

A Knight fall.

Q What do you call a bird of prey who cries all the time?

A A bawling eagle.

HA! HA! HA! HA! HA! HA! HA! HA! HA! HA!

86

The top of a loggerhead turtle's shell is heart-shaped.

KNOCK, KNOCK.

Who's there?
Water.
Water who?
Water you doing?

A group of
alligators is called
a congregation.

What kind of photos do alligators take?

Snapshots.

The Inuit name for a polar bear is *nanook*.

What's a
polar
bear's
favorite math problem?

Calculator

ON OFF

MRC M

7

4

1

0

.

+

Ice cubed.

Q

What's it called when you are surrounded by **sharks?**

A A vicious circle.

Q What does a lawyer wear to work?

A A law suit.

Q What's a blizzard's favorite game?

A Freeze tag

TONGUE TWISTER!

Say this fast three times:

A raccoon relaxed on racks of rackets.

91

BIG FLOWER:
What's up, Bud?

LITTLE FLOWER:
I'm busy blooming.

BIG FLOWER:
I'll leaf you alone.

Q

What do
boat captains
and
hat makers
worry about?

Capsizing.

A

Q What do you get when you
cross St. Nick with a crab?

Sandy claws. **A**

What do you get when you cross a **curly dog** with a **cinnamon cookie?**

Poodles were originally bred to retrieve waterfowl for hunters.

A snicker-poodle.

93

Camels store fat in their humps to provide energy when they don't have access to enough food.

KNOCK, KNOCK.

Who's there?
Adam's not.
Adam's not who?
Adam's not is dripping from his nose!

94

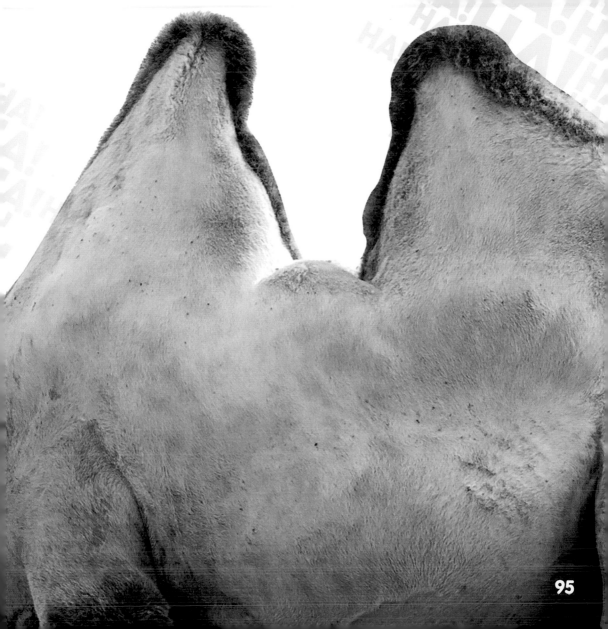

Say this fast three times:

Twelve toads

told tall tales.

Although most black bears are black, some are cinnamon-brown, silvery-blue, or white.

KNOCK,

KNOCK.

Who's there?
Cattle.
Cattle who?
Cattle chase the mouse away.

Q What do you get when you cross ice cream with an angry ape?

A Grrr-rilla.

Q Why does the chef **laugh** when she cooks **breakfast?**

A Because the egg always cracks a yolk.

Q What's it called when you run into a sprinting cheetah?

A A speed bump.

TONGUE TWISTER!

Say this fast three times:

Gnats gnaw nuts.

Q Who does an insect call to repair its house?

A A carpenter ant.

Q What did the **guitar player** do to get his car out of the mud?

A He rocked and rolled it.

100

When threatened, the short-horned chameleon raises its earflaps to look larger.

KNOCK, KNOCK.
Who's there?
Popover.
Popover who?
Popover later for some ice cream.

What do you get when you cross popcorn,

a hot dog,
and
a
stack
of books?

Kernel Mustard in the library.

Geckos, including these leopard geckos, have the best eyesight of any lizard species studied.

KNOCK, KNOCK.

Who's there?
Marionette.
Marionette who?
Marionette the last piece of pie.

Q What do you get when you cross a tissue and a cook?

A A handker-chef.

Q What did the **police officers** do when they crashed their car into a bakery?

A They made copcakes.

Q Where do **twin leeches** go on the **Internet?**

A To a para-site.

Q What's a computer mouse's favorite snack?

A Microchips.

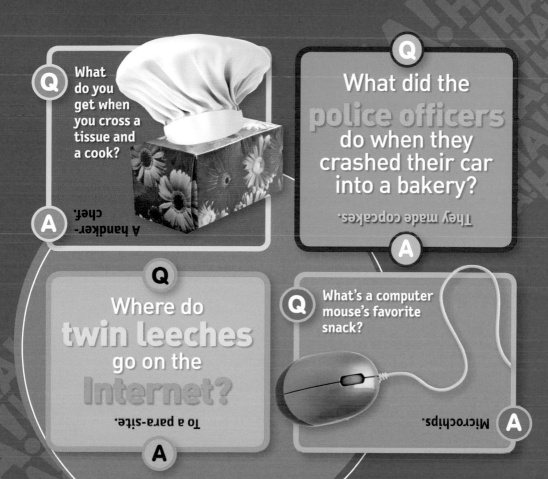

105

Q What do you get when you cross an ATM machine and a bovine?

A A cash cow.

Q Why can't the mountaintop sit next to anyone during a test?

A It always gets caught peaking.

Q Why don't **Saturday** and **Sunday** ever get picked to play tug-of-war?

A Because they're always the weekend.

Q How does a reptile tune the radio?

A Croc-a-dials.

What do you call a
comic book character
who ate too many donuts?

A supersized hero!

KNOCK, KNOCK.

Who's there?
Pickle.
Pickle who?
Pickle come in handy to get the lock open.

108

Q How do you write a letter on the ocean floor?

A Use sandpaper.

Q What's the **grumpiest** thing in your yard?

A Crab grass.

Koalas are often mistakenly called bears, but they are actually marsupials.

110

A pair of lovebirds will bond for life.

111

Q What did the stressed-out toad get?

A Worry warts.

Q What's a **sea monster's** favorite kind of sandwich?

A A sub.

The red fox is the largest fox species.

HA!HA!HA!HA!HA!HA!HA!HA!

112

KNOCK,
KNOCK.

Who's there?
Mikey.
Mikey who?
Mikey doesn't work. Can
you open the door?

Why didn't the boot believe the floor mat?

Because the mat lied like a rug.

A sheep may recognize the faces of other sheep in its herd.

KNOCK, KNOCK.

Who's there?
Acute.
Acute who?
Acute puppy wants you to come out and play.

Say this fast three times:

Cheap ship trip.

Q Where do minivans swim?

A In the carpool.

117

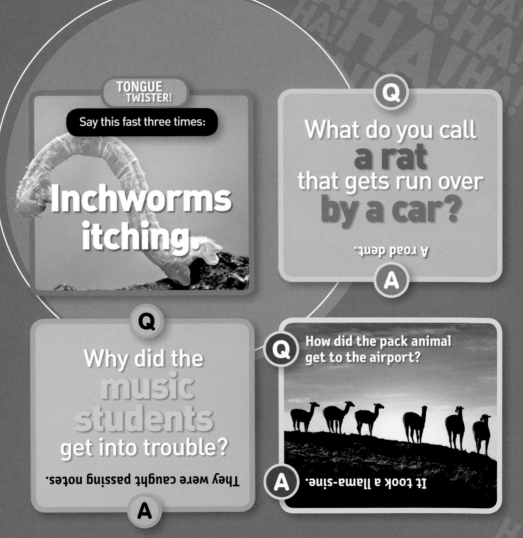

Inchworms itching.

Q

What do you call **a rat** that gets run over **by a car?**

A A road dent.

Q

Why did the **music students** get into trouble?

A They were caught passing notes.

Q How did the pack animal get to the airport?

A It took a llama-sine.

What's the **funniest place** to wait for a soft drink **at a party?**

The punch line.

When the patriot crab buries itself in sand, it sticks out its eyestalks to see.

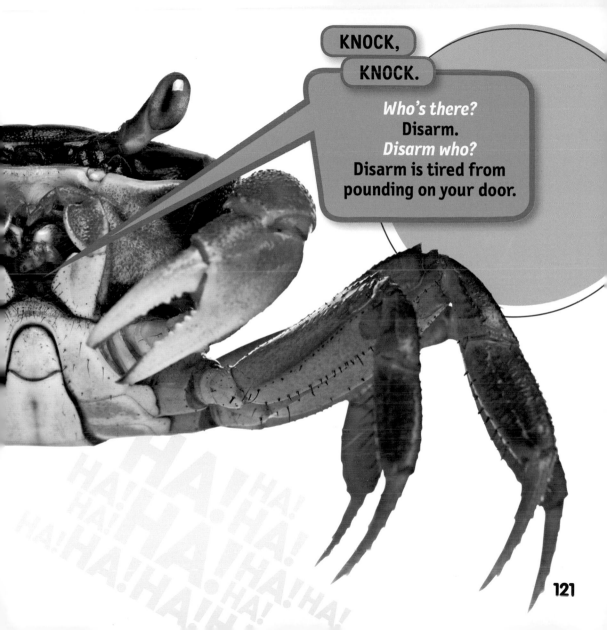

121

The emu's name comes from an old Arabic word that means "large bird."

KNOCK, KNOCK.

Who's there?
Stormy.
Stormy who?
Stormy skateboard in the garage, will ya?

GOLFER 1:
You better stay away from George today.

GOLFER 2:
Why?

GOLFER 1:
He's teed off.

Q What's it called when space rocks land on one side of the outfield?

A A meteor-right field.

Q

Why did the sci-fi fan wrap her car in herbs?

She loved thyme travel.

A

Q What happens when you leave the garbage outside in France?

A You get French fries.

Q Who do you call for underwater repairs?

A A sawfish and a hammerhead.

Q Where does a dog go to get a new tail?

A A retail store.

Q What kind of ring does a fry cook give his girlfriend?

A An onion ring.

Why did
the
thief
who stole a
loaf
of rye
go to
jail?

He was caught bread-handed.

125

What's it called when you remove half the rabbits

from a field?

A haircut.

Born with a black coat, this female elephant seal soon sheds and grows a new gray coat.

KNOCK, KNOCK.

Who's there?
Seaweed.
Seaweed who?
Seaweed be there by now if you hadn't taken a wrong turn.

128

Q Why couldn't the lock sleep?

A It was all keyed up.

TONGUE TWISTER!

Say this fast three times:

Greek grapes.

129

TEACHER: Don't you dare tell me the dog ate your homework!

JEREMY: Nah, that excuse is so old, my grandpa used it.

TEACHER: Good. Now, where's your homework?

JEREMY: I don't have it, my mouse took too many bytes out of it.

Q What do you call an unlucky psychic?

A An unfortunate teller.

Q Why did the beekeeper quit his job?

A He kept getting hives.

A swamp rabbit sometimes hides from predators underwater, keeping only its nose above water to breathe.

KNOCK, KNOCK.

Who's there?
Kayak.
Kayak who?
Kayak with you about something?

Tree frogs have sticky disks on their fingers and toes that help them climb on leaves.

KNOCK, KNOCK.

Who's there?
Mummify.
Mummify who?
Mummify clean my room, may I go to the mall?

133

Say this fast three times:

Camille's camera captured a camouflaged camel.

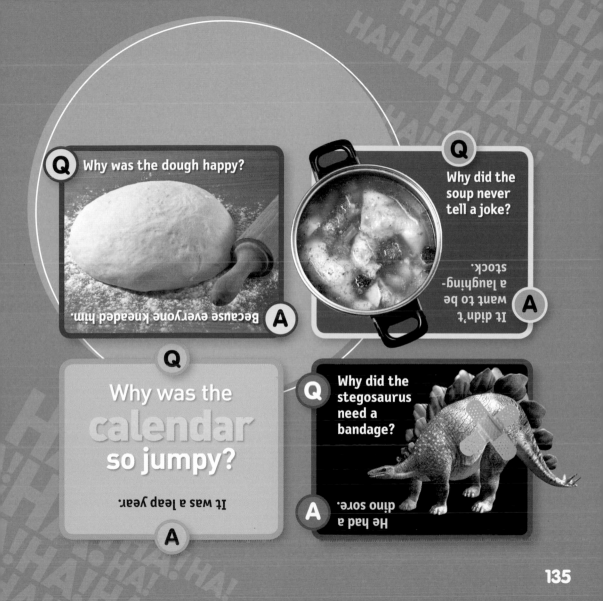

Q Why was the dough happy?

A Because everyone kneaded him.

Q Why did the soup never tell a joke?

A It didn't want to be a laughing-stock.

Q Why was the **calendar** so jumpy?

A It was a leap year.

Q Why did the stegosaurus need a bandage?

A He had a dino sore.

Say this fast three times:

Alice asks for axes.

Oriental small-clawed otters use at least a dozen calls to communicate.

Q Why was the strawberry in trouble?

A It was always in a jam.

136

KNOCK, KNOCK.

Who's there?
Target.
Target who?
Target on your shoe, and now you're stuck to the floor.

137

What do you get when you cross a fish and a judge?

The scales of justice.

KNOCK,
KNOCK.

Who's there?
Leasing.
Leasing who?
Leasings off-key.

The great gray owl
dives headfirst into
the snow to catch
voles, mouselike
rodents that
burrow in the snow.

Q Why did the bike appear on television?

A It was a good spokesperson.

Q Why was the worm found guilty of robbery?

A It didn't have a leg to stand on.

Q Where do cheeseburgers get to know each other?

A At a meat and greet.

Q What text message would you get from a hyena?

A lol.

141

Q When is traffic like an infant?

A When it crawls.

Q What did the boy say when he was accused of tying his dad's shoelaces together?

A Knot true.

Q Where do cats wait to pay their bills?

A The fee line.

TONGUE TWISTER!

Say this fast three times:

Much-mashed mushrooms.

142

What made the
deck of cards
disappear?

It got lost in the shuffle.

143

Elephants sometimes entwine their trunks to greet each other.

KNOCK, KNOCK.

Who's there?
Housefly.
Housefly who?
Housefly right over her head in the tornado.

Did you hear about the little birds that started an airline?

They had cheep flights.

147

A chimpanzee often makes a different nest to sleep in each night.

KNOCK, KNOCK.

Who's there?
Summon.
Summon who?
Summon down the street is looking for you.

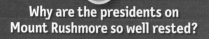

Q

Why are the presidents on
Mount Rushmore so well rested?

They sleep like rocks.

A

Q What type of
music
does a gumball
listen to?

Bubble rap.

A

149

Q What does a firefly order at a restaurant?

A A light meal.

Q Why did the **patient** with **amnesia** go for a **run?**

A To jog her memory.

Q What do **puzzles** say when they **fight?**

A Crosswords.

TONGUE TWISTER!

Say this fast three times:

Ted texts Tess in Texas.

150

HA! HA! HA! HA! HA!

How does a ghost lock its door?

With a dead bolt.

151

Friendly Frank flips fine flapjacks.

The round structure on a beluga whale's head is called a melon.

KNOCK, KNOCK.

Who's there?
Classify.
Classify who?
Classify promise no homework, will you please pay attention?

Q Why did the eye doctor's kid refuse to be seen with him?

A He always made a spectacle of himself.

Q Why was the faucet moody?

A Because it always ran hot and cold.

Q Why was the orange afraid of the mobsters?

A They tried to put the squeeze on it!

Q What does a hairless cat wear to a party?

A Its birthday suit.

Q Why did the **muffler** quit the **car business?**

A It was exhausted.

Q What do you call a fairy godmother who can't make decisions?

A Wishy-washy.

KNOCK, KNOCK.

Who's there?
Distaste.
Distaste who?
Distaste terrible!

A dusky leaf monkey utters a loud call to say, "Get off my turf!"

157

KNOCK, KNOCK.

Who's there?
Trainee.
Trainee who?
Trainee was trying
to catch left
ten minutes ago.

158

Lion cubs are born blind. They begin to see when they are about one week old.

TONGUE TWISTER!

Say this fast three times:

Eleven lemons.

Q Why didn't anyone trust the salmon?

A They smelled something fishy.

Q What do you call your shoes when you walk on ice?

A Slippers

Q Why did everyone avoid talking to the cook at the barbecue restaurant?

A She was always grilling people

Q Where does a penguin go to the movies?

A At the dive in.

Q Why do astronauts look forward to liftoff?

A Because it's always a blast!

Q What's it called when a dog runs a long way to retrieve a ball?

A Far-fetched.

Domestic pigs—usually raised on farms—have curly tails. Wild pigs have straight tails.

HA!HA!HA!HA!HA!HA!HA!HA!HA!HA!

KNOCK, KNOCK.

Who's there?
Internet.
Internet who?
Internet is where the basketball goes.

163

If two witches were watching two watches, which witch would watch which watch?

165

Elephant seals are named for the trunklike snout that extends from the male's head.

KNOCK, KNOCK.

Who's there?
Havasu.
Havasu who?
Havasu call me!

TONGUE TWISTER!

Say this fast three times.

Seven Sasquatches squashed Sasha.

What did the musical tires name their rock group? **Q**

The Rubber Band. **A**

167

The Chinese
name for panda
is *daxiongmao*,
which means
"large bear-cat."

KNOCK, KNOCK.

Who's there?
Erode.
Erode who?
Erode into town on a donkey.

169

Q What instrument does **Dumbo** play?

A An eardrum.

Q Why was the grizzly turned away from the restaurant?

A No bear feet allowed.

Q Who keeps putting beards on dogs?

A The Dog Whiskerer.

Q Why didn't the veterinarian want to treat the toad?

A She was afraid it would croak.

170

Why did the **android** remove his hard drive?

Because he wanted to change his mind.

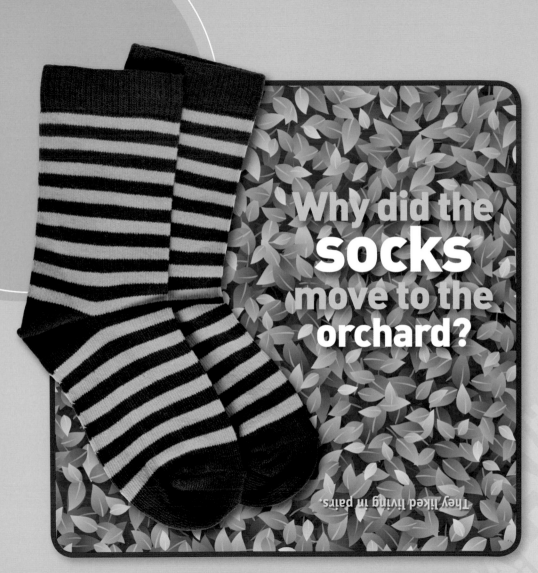

Why did the **socks** move to the orchard?

They liked living in pairs.

Q How do you know when water gets mad?

A It sits and steams.

Q What always has its hands in front of its face?

A A clock.

Q Why did the painter feel cold?

A She forgot to put on a second coat.

TONGUE TWISTER!

Say this fast three times:

Rough Ralph raffled ruffles.

Q What happens when you interrupt a karate master's breakfast?

A Snap, crackle, chop!

Q Did you hear about the drummer with the bad heart?

A He couldn't keep a beat.

Q How does a mother eagle punish a naughty eaglet?

A She grounds her.

Q What do you call a **best seller** written on a **cell phone?**

A A txt bk.

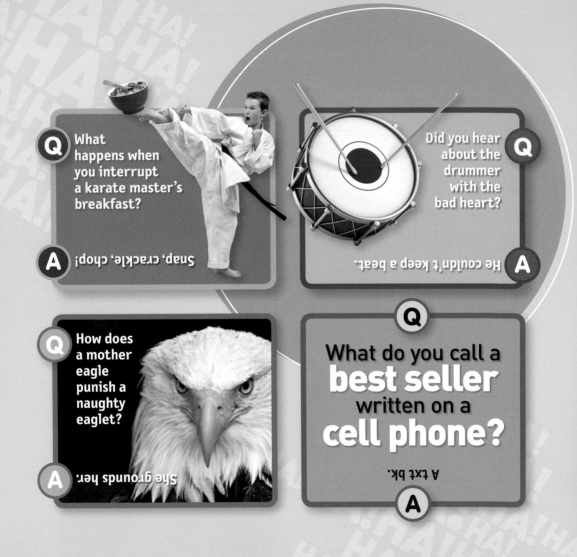

174

Spoonbills use their spoon-shaped beaks to snatch up fish and other small aquatic creatures.

KNOCK,

KNOCK.

Who's there?
Isolate.
Isolate who?
Isolate you're already in your pajamas.

175

Why did the mop sign up for a self-defense class?

Because everyone tried to wipe the floor with it.

Red pandas like to sleep with their tails wrapped around their heads.

KNOCK, KNOCK.

Who's there?
Aboard.
Aboard who?
Aboard is missing from your front porch.

Q What does a Martian call his patio?

A Outer space.

Q Why did the man's bed disappear?

A It went undercover.

179

Q How did the door react to bad news?

A It became unhinged.

DETECTIVE: Rover, you're the one who's been tearing up the neighbor's shoes!

ROVER: How did you catch me?

DETECTIVE: If the chew fits...

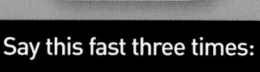

TONGUE TWISTER!

Say this fast three times:

I love unique New York.

Female iguanas are attracted to males with long, healthy spines on their backs.

KNOCK, KNOCK.

Who's there?
Wafer.
Wafer who?
Wafer me, I'm almost ready.

KNOCK, KNOCK.

Who's there?
Bulldozing.
Bulldozing who?
Bulldozing on your lawn,
don't wake him up!

A group of capuchins is called a barrel of monkeys or a troop.

The two-toed tree toad tried to tread where the three-toed tree toad trod.

Q

Why did the man buy
plane tickets
for a bunch of
hogs?

A His boss said he could have a raise when pigs fly.

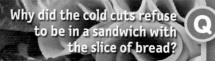

Why did the cold cuts refuse to be in a sandwich with the slice of bread? **Q**

A The bread was a real heel.

Q Where can you dig up a good joke?

A On a funny farm.

Why did the boy think he was psychic when he found change in his pocket? **Q**

A Because he discovered that he had six cents.

Q What did the snowman do when he got mad?

A He had a meltdown.

Q What did the cranky man say to the flower vendor?

A Go petal your stuff somewhere else.

Cats can be right-pawed or left-pawed.

KNOCK, KNOCK.

Who's there?
Yell.
Yell who?
WHHHOOOO!

TONGUE TWISTER!

Say this fast three times:

This is a zither.

A zither is a stringed instrument that a musician often plays while holding the instrument in his lap.

Like all reptiles, this sand lizard can't produce its own body heat. It basks in the sun to keep warm.

KNOCK,
KNOCK.

Who's there?
Shhh.
Shhh who?
Stop shooing me away!
That's rude.

Q Why was the cliff such a great poker player?

A It knew how to bluff.

Q What's the friendliest thing in a parade?

A A flag—it's always waving.

Q Why was the **cemetery owner** so **paranoid?**

A He saw plots everywhere!

Q Why did the mallard stick its head under the water?

A It heard someone yell "Duck!"

Q

How did the **cat** get a **drink** from the **Milky Way?**

A It used the Big Dipper.

Q Why did the library have to be fumigated?

A It was full of bookworms.

Q Why were the computers afraid of the guy with a bad cold?

A He was always hacking.

Q

What do you call a **pretty woman** who flees from a **fashion show?**

A A runaway model.

The shoebill is named for its large beak, which is shaped like a pointy shoe.

KNOCK, KNOCK.

Who's there?
Ahead.
Ahead who?
Ahead of a monster just peaked over your shoulder.

A rhinoceros's horn and human fingernails are made from similar substances.

HA!HA!HA!HA!HA!HA!HA!

195

The oldest male lions in a pride often have the darkest manes.

KNOCK, KNOCK.

Who's there?
Samurai.
Samurai who?
Samurai will pick you up in an hour.

Q

Why was the bandleader not allowed to drive a train?

A

He was a bad conductor.

TONGUE TWISTER!

Say this fast three times:

Jack's knapsack strap snapped.

197

Say this fast three times:

Six thick thistle sticks.

Q Where do cardboard cartons fight each other?

A In a boxing ring.

Q What does an **artist** use to hold up his **pants?**

A A drawstring.

198

Why did the **girl** put on a **lampshade?**

She was feeling light-headed.

She was feeling light-headed.

HA! HA! HA! HA!

Otters close their eyes
and nostrils when they
dive underwater.

KNOCK, KNOCK.

Who's there?
Weave.
Weave who?
Weave been telling too many knock knock jokes!

JOKEFINDER

203

JOKEFINDER

Story jokes

Tongue twisters

ILLUSTRATIONCREDITS

Published by the National Geographic Society
John M. Fahey, Jr., *Chairman of the Board and Chief Executive Officer*
Timothy T. Kelly, *President*
Declan Moore, *Executive Vice President; President, Publishing*
Melina Gerosa Bellows, *Executive Vice President; Chief Creative Officer,*
 Books, Kids, and Family

Prepared by the Book Division
Hector Sierra, *Senior Vice President and General Manager*
Nancy Laties Feresten, *Senior Vice President, Kids Publishing and Media*
Jonathan Halling, *Design Director, Books and Children's Publishing*
Jay Sumner, *Director of Photography, Children's Publishing*
Jennifer Emmett, *Vice President, Editorial Director, Children's Books*
Eva Absher-Schantz, *Design Director, Kids Publishing and Media*
Carl Mehler, *Director of Maps*
R. Gary Colbert, *Production Director*
Jennifer A. Thornton, *Director of Managing Editorial*

Staff for This Book
Robin Terry, *Project Editor*
David M. Seager, *Art Director*
Lisa Jewell, *Illustrations Editor*
Ruthie Thompson, *Designer*
Nancy Honovich, *Researcher*
Kate Olesin, *Associate Editor*
Kathryn Robbins, *Associate Designer*
Hillary Moloney, *Illustrations Assistant*
Grace Hill, *Associate Managing Editor*
Joan Gossett, *Production Editor*
Lewis R. Bassford, *Production Manager*
Susan Borke, *Legal and Business Affairs*

Manufacturing and Quality Management
Phillip L. Schlosser, *Senior Vice President*
Chris Brown, *Vice President, NG Book Manufacturing*
George Bounelis, *Vice President, Production Services*
Nicole Elliott, *Manager*
Rachel Faulise, *Manager*
Robert L. Barr, *Manager*

Based on the "Just Joking" department in
***National Geographic Kids* magazine**

CELEBRATING
‹125›
YEARS

The National Geographic Society is one of the world's largest nonprofit scientific and educational organizations. Founded in 1888 to "increase and diffuse geographic knowledge," the Society works to inspire people to care about the planet. National Geographic reflects the world through its magazines, television programs, films, music and radio, books, DVDs, maps, exhibitions, live events, school publishing programs, interactive media and merchandise. *National Geographic* magazine, the Society's official journal, published in English and 33 local-language editions, is read by more than 38 million people each month. The National Geographic Channel reaches 320 million households in 34 languages in 166 countries. National Geographic Digital Media receives more than 15 million visitors a month. National Geographic has funded more than 9,400 scientific research, conservation and exploration projects and supports an education program promoting geography literacy. For more information, visit nationalgeographic.com.

For more information, please call 1-800-NGS LINE (647-5463) or write to the following address:
National Geographic Society
1145 17th Street N.W.
Washington, D.C. 20036-4688 U.S.A.

Visit us online at nationalgeographic.com/books

For librarians and teachers: ngchildrensbooks.org

More for kids from National Geographic: kids.nationalgeographic.com

For information about special discounts for bulk purchases, please contact National Geographic Books Special Sales: ngspecsales@ngs.org

For rights or permissions inquiries, please contact National Geographic Books Subsidiary Rights: ngbookrights@ngs.org

Library of Congress Cataloging-in-Publication Data

Just joking 3: 300 hilarious jokes about everything, including tongue twisters, riddles, and more! / National Geographic Society.
 p. cm.
 Includes index.
 ISBN 978-1-4263-1098-0 (pbk. : alk. paper) -- ISBN 978-1-4263-1099-7 (library binding : alk. paper)
 1. Wit and humor, Juvenile. I. National Geographic Society (U.S.)
 PN6166.J663 2013
 818'.60208--dc23
                  2012026528

Printed in China

13/PPS/2